Vibrant Spirituality

Vibrant Spirituality

10 READY-TO-USE MEETINGS

Jenny Baker

Cover design by 4-9-0 ltd
Typeset by Temple Design
Print Management by Adare Carwin

WITH THANKS TO:

Jonny, Joel and Harry Baker; Jason Gardner for timely ideas; Ali Hull for skilful editing; John Buckeridge and Steve Adams at Youthwork magazine for encouragement and opportunities to write.

Contents

Introduction

Youth workers are as diverse as the young people that they work with, but *Vibrant Spirituality* is based on a few assumptions that I believe are fairly common.

- You share the huge privilege and responsibility of introducing young people to Jesus and helping them grow in their faith.

- You are committed to your group, but are busy – willing to do what it takes to help young people grow, but with not a lot of time to do it in.

- You know your group and are used to adapting resources to suit the individuals that you work with.

- You're not an expert in every area that you want to cover, but you want to learn with young people as you help them explore key issues.

Vibrant Spirituality offers you material to teach the Christian faith and help young people grow in their relationships with Jesus in a way that engages them and doesn't lecture them. It includes ready-to-use guides with extra sheets on the CDROM, to cut down on preparation time. It includes discussion starters on each topic to provide a different route in, or as an alternative to an activity in the ready-to-use guide. It gives you the opportunity to think through what you believe, offering suggestions for where to find out more about the subject and extra stories, websites, Bible passages and sources to find the adaptations that you'll need to make.

Under each topic you'll find the following:

INTRODUCTION

This section will help you to prepare for the session that you'll lead with the group, and provides extra ideas and sources of information to enable you to tailor the ready-to-use guide to your group. You'll find suggestions for Bible passages to read, films or CDs that are relevant to the topic, websites to find out more information, important statistics, quotes from well-known figures, suggestions of books to read, and questions to think about. Start here and you'll be able to think through your own views on the topic before addressing it with your group.

DISCUSSION STARTER

Each topic has a discussion starter – either a film clip, a song to listen to, or a summary of a news story – all with discussion questions to use with your group, providing a different, more informal way of addressing the topic. The discussion starter can be used in addition to the main outline, or to replace one of the suggested activities in it, or it can be used on its own for a shorter session. On the whole, older teenagers enjoy discussing issues, while younger teenagers enjoy activities, although there are always exceptions to the rule. The ready-to-use outlines are biblically based and explicitly Christian; on the whole the discussion starters aren't and can be used in any context. You can, of course, use some of the Bible passages and suggestions in the main outline to lead the discussion more explicitly on to matters of faith. I've indicated where a video clip contains swearing; watch it and decide whether it's appropriate for your group. The video clips and CD tracks are from classic films and CDs and should be relevant for a while yet. For information and Christian comment on the latest films, CDs and books, visit the Damaris website www.culturewatch.org

ON THE CDROM

The CDROM contains sheets to be used in the sessions, some of which can be adapted by you. Don't worry; this is not a death-by-worksheet resource. Many of the sheets contain Bible study references and questions to hand out among your group, or details of role-plays, or quizzes or information for games. No more scribbling down references or instructions from the book to hand out to young people; this resource has done it all for you. A few of the sheets can be given to each member of the group to work on, but only where it's helpful, and never for the sake of it. A section with each topic tells you exactly which sheets are needed for the ready-to-use guide and how many of each you need to produce.

GET READY

This provides a handy list of all the preparation you need to do for the ready-to-use guide in the book. You'll be able to see just how much work is required and how far in advance you need to do it. But that doesn't mean you have to do it all. Try to involve young people in preparing and leading; they may well learn more by being given responsibility for part of the session.

A READY-TO-USE GUIDE

Each topic has a complete biblically based meeting outline including ice-breakers, discussion starters, games, creative Bible study ideas, role-plays, worship and prayer suggestions and more. If your group is comfortable singing, then add this in but it is not prescribed very often, as many groups either lack musicians or else singing causes embarrassment. The meeting guides give young people the opportunity to discuss their opinions, analyse their beliefs, find out what the Bible says and decide how they want to live. Feel free to play around with this outline and make it your own.

Giving

This is the first in a series of three sessions on Matthew 6 looking at the subjects of giving, forgiving and fasting. Jesus clearly expects his listeners to do all three, saying 'when you...', not 'if'. He talks about the need to develop a secret spirituality that has depth and is not done to impress others. It's not a contradiction to discuss this in a group situation as you can talk about the issues and give space for young people to decide on their own how they will put them into practice. The sessions can be done individually or as a series of three.

● For each of these three sessions, you need to think about your own spirituality and how you nurture your relationship with God. Not that you have to be sorted and perfect before you can talk to young people about it, but it will really help them if you can share your own experiences and what has helped you. Don't feel that you have to make yourself more vulnerable than you feel comfortable with. So for this first session, think about giving. Who do you give to? How do you decide how much to give away? What stops you giving more? What stories do you have to tell of God's provision for you?

● Official surveys show young people to be the least likely to give to charity, but is that the whole picture? The Charity's Aid Foundation did some research into young people aged 16 to 24 and giving to charity which was published in November 2002. There is a summary of their findings on the Joseph Rowntree Foundation website www.jrf.org.uk/knowledge/findings/socialpolicy/n22.asp. The Giving Campaign did research into giving among 11 to 16 year olds and have set up a new website based on their findings www.g-nation.co.uk. They found that this younger age group is very engaged in giving through formal mechanisms and through schools. Is that true for your group? How much do they give of their own money? How much of their fund-raising is about getting others to give through being sponsored? And what else do they give apart from money in terms of time, effort and commitment?

1

Discussion starter   PIN THE CHEQUE ON THE DONKEY

In recent years, charities have faced some difficult times. There's talk of recession and wars, worry about house prices, job security and pensions – and all of that makes people less likely to give to charity. They want to hang onto their hard-earned cash for themselves. But there's one charity that doesn't seem to have to worry about money – the Donkey Sanctuary in Devon. Last year they were given £13 million – more than Age Concern and the Samaritans.

The Donkey Sanctuary was set up by a woman called Elisabeth Svendsen in 1969 after she got her first donkey called Naughty Face. Now the Sanctuary looks after 3,500 donkeys on its farm and has another 1,500 in its donkey-fostering scheme. These are looked after by families around the UK who are able to meet the high standards of accommodation required. The Donkey Sanctuary looks after nearly three-quarters of the UK donkey population and it means we have probably the best looked-after donkeys in the world.

People in Britain are well known for giving more to animal charities than to children's charities. 'When people make disparaging comments about animal charities, what they are making disparaging comments about really is the British public, 'says Tom Monk who works for a charity marketing group. 'What's quite hard to swallow is the fact that lots of people out there would rather give money and sympathy to donkeys than to, for example, the children of refugees, or other hard-to-support causes.'

Source: The Guardian, 18 Feruary 2003

- Why do you think so many people give money to The Donkey Sanctuary and to other animal charities? Why are they less likely to give money to charities working with refugees and asylum seekers?

- What charities have you given money to, or raised money for? Why did you decide to support that charity?

- What reasons or excuses do people have for not giving to charity? How would you answer those excuses?

- Why do Christians think giving is an important thing to do?

ON THE CDROM

- Giving sheet one – reasons why people don't give money

GET READY

- Make one copy of Giving sheet one from the CDROM and cut into strips.

- Get a couple of young people to rehearse the sketch on God's generosity. You'll need a large sheet and the means to secure it across the corner of the room, a spring onion and a leek, a table tennis ball and a football, a hanky and a sheet, and a bucket of water or shredded paper, depending on what your room can take.

- You could get some information about local or international projects that work with people in need to show how much difference even a relatively small amount of money can make to people who are poor.

- You will also need celebrity magazines, Bibles, pens, about 40 clothes pegs, writing paper and envelopes.

READY-TO-USE GUIDE

AIMS: *to look at the need to develop a secret spirituality*
To encourage young people into the habit of giving.

SERIES INTRO – SHOW OFFS!

Have a selection of celebrity magazines. Split your group into twos. Each pair should choose a celebrity and construct a case for why they should be awarded the 'Show Off of the Year' award. Give them a minute to present their case, and then vote for which celebrity is the best at self-publicity.

Young people are encouraged to have a healthy self-esteem. What's the difference between that and being a show-off?

GIVE, FORGIVE, FAST

Make the link to this series of meetings. In Jesus' day people were showing off how spiritual they were, wanting everyone to see their 'acts of righteousness' and expecting people to be impressed. People would hire trumpeters who went ahead of them into the temple and made sure everyone was there to see them give their donations. Jesus addresses the need for us to develop a secret spirituality through three specific practices – giving, forgiving and fasting. Read Matthew 6:1-18 (the CEV actually uses the word show-offs). Get them to look at verses 2-4, 5-6 and 16-18 in particular. Jesus gives similar advice about all three issues – can they pick out five things common to all three passages?

● Jesus says 'when' you give, pray which includes forgiving, fast – not 'if'.

● Don't be hypocritical or a show-off.

● If you do these things to be seen by other people, that's all the reward you'll get.

● Giving, forgiving and fasting should be done secretly.

● God will see you and reward you.

TEAMS OF INDIVIDUALS

Brainstorm a list of activities that take place in groups or teams – sports, quizzes, bands, rescue teams. What type of individual is needed on those teams? Someone who knows their stuff as an individual, who trains hard, who can be relied on. As Christians we need to express our spirituality – the way we live out our faith – both in groups and on our own. It's great to get together and pray, worship or study the Bible. But if that's the only place that we do those things, we are missing out on getting to know God intimately. In these passages Jesus encourages his followers to develop a secret relationship with God – to do things that only God and you will know about. How will this benefit the whole youth group?

ON TO GIVING

Ask for six volunteers and give each of them six clothes pegs that they then peg on their clothes. Give them three minutes to get rid of their pegs by pegging them onto other players – at the same time they have to avoid being pegged themselves. Players can only hold one peg in their hands at a time and if they miss-peg and it falls to the floor, they have to pick it up and try to peg someone else. After three minutes the winner is the player with the fewest pegs – the one who was most successful at giving things away!

DISCUSS

How easy do they find it to give – you could ask what was the last time they gave something away without someone asking for it? What resources have they got that they could give away – time, money, talents, friendship? What causes have they given to in the past? Have they been involved in any fund-raising initiatives? What would they do if they were given loads of money? You don't want to ask them to boast about their giving, but try to find out about their attitudes and experiences. Be aware that some young people may have very little materially, so don't just focus on giving away money.

I'D LOVE TO GIVE BUT...

Jesus said 'When you give...' so it's not an optional extra. However, it's very easy to find excuses! Hand out the excuses from the CDROM to the group. Ask people to come up with arguments about why this person should still give.

● I'd love to give to people in need but I'm completely broke

● I think people should look after themselves – I don't expect handouts from anyone

● Once I've saved enough for a PlayStation 2, I'll give some money away

● I haven't got as much money as Bernard. Ask him to give something

● Once I'm earning a salary, I'll start giving to charity

Can they think of any other excuses that people might use? How would they answer those? This discussion counteracts any excuses they may have themselves without putting anyone on the spot.

5

GOD'S GENEROSITY

This illustrates God's generosity. Get a couple of young people to help you set it up before the meeting and act it out. Set up a sheet across one corner of the room with one person hidden behind it, and one person in front. Explain that God multiplies what we give to him so that he will never be in debt to us. The person in front of the sheet throws over a spring onion – back comes a leek. Over goes a table tennis ball – back comes a football. Over goes a hanky – back comes a sheet. For the final item, the person in front spits (or pretends to!) over the top of the sheet and back comes a bucket of water. (If your room won't take water on the floor, get the person behind the sheet to charge out with a bucket as if to throw it over everyone – it can be full of shredded paper instead.) Read Luke 6:38 to the group. Ask them to think of all the things that God has given to them – God is so amazingly generous to us. Encourage them to be generous people and to get into the habit of giving early in their lives. It doesn't suddenly become easier once they have more money.

LETTER TO MYSELF

Give everyone an envelope and piece of writing paper. Invite them to write a letter to themselves in which they reflect on what they have learned this week and how they are going to put it into practice. How generous are they? What have they got that they can give? Who do they want to give to? Stress that this letter is for their eyes only. Once it is written they should seal it in the envelope and write their own name on the front. Tell them that in the next couple of sessions you will be looking at forgiveness and then fasting. In each of those sessions they will have an opportunity to add to their letters. Finish with prayer, asking God to bless the decisions they have made.

Forgiveness

Forgiveness is quite an alien concept in our society – it is generally accepted that we have a right to revenge and compensation and that people should be made to pay for their crimes. For this reason, it may be quite a difficult concept for young people to grasp – it seems a crazy thing to do to forgive someone who has hurt you. Be prepared for lots of discussion and help them to realise the enormity of God's forgiveness for them.

● Some amazing stories of forgiveness came out of the Truth and Reconciliation Committee (TRC) that was set up in South Africa by the government after the end of apartheid. All sections of society suffered from conflict and human rights abuses and the aim of the TRC was to listen to what had happened, to help South Africans come to terms with their past and work towards reconciliation. The register of reconciliation on the site contains some very moving words. Archbishop Desmond Tutu was appointed head of the commission and you can read his statement in the 1995 Press release section of the website www.doj.gov.za/trc/ He makes good links between reconciliation, forgiveness, repentance and truth.

● Spend some time thinking about your relationships with other people. Is there anyone that you need to forgive? Do you need to do anything to repair any broken relationships? If you have struggled to forgive someone, or still struggle, think about how appropriate it is to share that with the group and how much you can say.

Some Bible passages:

Luke 23:32-43 *Jesus doesn't ask us to do what he could not do himself. He speaks words of forgiveness to those who are crucifying him and to the criminal next to him.*

7

Luke 7:36-50 *The woman who anoints Jesus' feet with perfume knows what real forgiveness is. What does Simon see when he looks at her? What does Jesus see?*

John 21:15-19 *Jesus shows he has forgiven Peter for his betrayal. He doesn't ask Peter 'are you sorry?' or 'how do I know I can trust you now?' What does he ask?*

Discussion starter

SAVING PRIVATE RYAN

Show a clip from the film *Saving Private Ryan* (cert 15) that demonstrates forgiveness in a difficult situation. The film is set in World War 2. John Miller, played by Tom Hanks, is a US army captain who is given the task of tracking down Private James Ryan, played by Matt Damon. Ryan's three brothers have all been killed in the war and the US government want to bring him home safely. Miller and his men come across a German radar post as they search for Ryan. The men want to ignore it and continue their search but Miller is determined to put it out of action. A gun battle follows and the Americans take control of the station, but one of them, Wayne, is shot and dies. There is one German soldier left alive, and the clip begins with the US soldiers hitting him in anger that their friend has died. They make him dig graves for all the soldiers who have been killed. Miller decides to let the German soldier go, even though most of his men want to kill him. The clip ends with a shot of Miller and his men burying the dead, their silhouettes against the skyline. The clip includes some swearing.

Clip start time: 1.27.30
Clip end time: 1:37.00
Clip duration: nine and a half minutes.

● What would you do if you were one of the US soldiers in the film? What reasons are there for killing the soldier? What reasons are there for letting him go? Why is forgiveness so difficult?

● Why do you think Miller got the German to dig the graves, and left the decision about what to do with him until later?

● Miller knows that killing the German will affect him badly – what words of his indicate this belief?

- How can unforgiveness affect our relationships with God and with other people? Which hurts us more, forgiving someone even if they have hurt us badly, or being unforgiving?

ON THE CDROM

- Forgiveness sheet one – verses from the Bible about forgiveness

GET READY

- **Very important** In this session you'll ask people to think about where they have been hurt and who they need to forgive. If someone is in an on-going situation of being hurt – for example being bullied or abused – they should not be told that they just need to forgive. The bullying or abuse needs to be addressed. Before this session, make sure you know about your church's child protection policy.

- Make one copy of Forgiveness sheet one from the CDROM and cut into three.

- Pack a couple of rucksacks full of clothes for 'Stuck in the mud'. They need to be nice and bulky but not too heavy.

- Get group members to research news stories in advance for 'In the news' or take copies of newspapers to the session.

- You'll need the letters that they wrote in the Giving session if you did that one first and new envelopes, or a sheet of writing paper and an envelope for everyone.

- Choose a suitable venue to do the 'Receiving Forgiveness' activity at the end. Make sure there are lots of stones around – if not, take some from your garden. Or get some pieces of paper if you're not going out to a lake or river.

- You will also need Bibles, pens, strips of paper and sellotape or glue sticks to make paper chains and marker pens.

READY-TO-USE GUIDE

AIM: *to consider the conditional nature of God's forgiveness*

To understand the importance of forgiving others and receiving forgiveness

ICEBREAKER

Start with the kids' game 'Stuck in the mud'. One person is 'it'. If they touch someone, that person is 'stuck in the mud' and has to stand still until another player crawls through their legs. Give two people a couple of rucksacks full of clothes to wear. The person who is 'it' tries to get everyone stuck in which case they have won! Every couple of minutes, swap who is 'it'.

IN THE NEWS

Introduce the theme of forgiveness. Discuss some recent news stories where people have been wronged or sinned against. You could get some group members to research a news story each, perhaps creating a collage of newspaper stories or clips of TV interviews. Choose crimes of different magnitudes – murder, theft, adultery or aggression. For each one ask the following question, using the facts or your imaginations:

● Who is the victim of this sin or crime?

● What is their reaction to the person who has committed the sin?

● What will compensate them for what has been done to them?

● Do you think they should forgive? Why or why not?

● How will they feel about it in a year's time? In five years time?

TWO-WAY FORGIVENESS

Split the group into twos and threes. Ask them to read Matthew 6:5-15 and summarise the passage in two sentences – one about prayer and one about forgiveness. Ask them to read them out to the rest of the group.

We often talk about the unconditional love of God – that he loves us no matter what we do. However, God's forgiveness is different. What stops God forgiving us? Link to the 'stuck in the mud' game. Not forgiving others means we get stuck. Why is it difficult to forgive others? Why do you think God made his forgiveness conditional?

WHAT DOES IT MEAN?

Brainstorm what it means to forgive someone. What needs to happen in order for forgiveness to take place? How does your forgiveness affect your future relationship with the person you are forgiving? Are some things easier to forgive than others? What do they think of these statements: 'You just need to forgive and forget'; 'forgiving someone is the same as saying the crime doesn't matter'.

Bring out the following points in the discussion: To forgive someone is to let go of revenge, hurt and bitterness, to re-open the possibility of relationship and to take a risk that things might go wrong in the future. 'Forgive and forget' is not always possible. You can truly forgive someone and still remember what happened. Forgiveness is not saying 'it doesn't matter' but it is saying 'I won't take revenge.'

What difference might forgiveness make to both the victim of the crime and the person who committed it?

SIN'S CONSEQUENCES

Now it's time to apply this talk about forgiveness to their personal situations. Decide whether you will do this as an open discussion or whether it would work better with your group for them just to think privately about the issues you raise. Remind them that it's best to talk in general terms about events in the past, rather being specific about other people's names and actions.

Use an example from your life and talk about the consequences of unforgiveness. For example, you and a friend argue and fall out; you don't talk to each other for weeks; when you see them you feel angry; you spread gossip about them because you feel so upset; they find out and hate you even more and so on.

Ask the group to think about situations where they have been sinned against and have found it difficult to forgive, or haven't been able to forgive. Invite them to write on slips of paper the sin and the consequences of it. The group should join these slips together with sellotape or glue sticks to make a paper chain.

Talk about how unforgiveness can weigh you down. Ask the people who wore the rucksacks in the game what it was like. Then talk about how unforgiveness can break the chain, using your own example. Talk about the practicalities of forgiving someone and as you do, break the links of the paper chain. Ask them to consider how they could forgive people who have hurt them. Acknowledge that sometimes this is very difficult and can take time – the first step is to realise that you need to forgive.

GOD'S FORGIVENESS

Explain that God does not grade sin, so that murder is more serious than lying, or adultery is more offensive than anger. All of us need forgiveness as much as the people who have committed the crimes you considered at the start of the session. We all fall short of God's perfection. (This is a difficult concept to grasp as we instinctively feel that some sins are worse than others.)

We can learn a lot about forgiveness from God's example. Hand out copies of the verses from the CDROM and ask three people to read them. Although it can be difficult to forgive, being able to forgive makes a huge difference. God is able to set them free from all their sin and forgive them entirely.

LETTER TO MYSELF

Hand back to them the letters that they wrote during the Giving session or give them a new envelope and piece of paper. Give them some space to reflect on what they have heard and what they are going to do about it. Invite them to add to their letters, and then seal it in a fresh envelope with their name on for you to look after until next time.

RECEIVING FORGIVENESS

Give everyone a stone and a marker pen. Go outside to stand beside a lake or a river. Ask the group to write the names of anyone they need to forgive on their stone. As they write they can pray, telling God that they choose to forgive this person, or want to be able to.

Then get them to stand holding their stone and think about all the things they need forgiveness for personally. Allow them some space to confess these to God privately.

Then on a count of three, everyone should throw their stone as high and as far as they can. Can they get the stones back? That is how God treats their sin – gone and forgiven – and how they need to treat the wrong that has been done to them. Pray together that they would know the full joy of God's forgiveness.

If you are not near water, or don't fancy trekking to a lake, invite people to write the names of those they want to forgive on pieces of paper, You can then burn these outside on a fire or barbecue.

Fasting

Fasting is perhaps one of the most neglected spiritual disciplines in our churches, although your experience may be different! Young people may have heard more about Muslims fasting during the month of Ramadan, or about the benefits of detoxing by fasting, or about David Blaine's 44-day fast in a Perspex box over the Thames, than they have about the tradition of fasting in the Christian church. And yet it is a practice found in all strands of the church throughout history. Today, some charismatic house churches emphasise the role that fasting plays in spiritual warfare. The Anglican and Catholic churches encourage people to fast during Lent in some way. The Eastern Orthodox Church has four main periods of fasting, in addition to Wednesdays and Fridays being days of fasting. So it's there, just waiting to be rediscovered!

● Do you fast regularly? What experiences of fasting have you had in your life? It doesn't matter if your answers to those questions are 'no' and 'none' – that doesn't disqualify you from doing this session. Just be honest with the group and approach the subject in terms of 'let's learn about this together.' On the other hand, if it is part of your spirituality, think about how you will share that with your group.

● Find out about Sawm, the practice of fasting during Ramadan which is one of the five pillars of Islam. Talk to Muslim colleagues or neighbours about their experience. The BBC website has some information www.bbc.co.uk/religion/religions/islam/customs/sawm/index.shtml and there is an article on the 24-7 prayer site www.24-7prayer.com; click on articles and do a search on fasting. What are the similarities and differences between Muslim fasting and a Christian view of fasting?

Some Bible passages:

Joel 2:12-13 *Here, fasting is part of repentance and shows a depth of feeling. Do we take repentance too lightly?*

Matthew 4:1-11 *Jesus fasted for 40 days and 40 nights. What happened just before and just after this period? What do you think fasting contributed to Jesus?*

Luke 18:9-14 *The Pharisee and the tax collector – another story to emphasise that fasting is not a reason for boasting.*

Discussion starter   A DRAMATIC WAY TO BE HEARD

Fasting has often been used as a way of protesting against injustice and as a means of applying political pressure. Abas Amini is an Iranian Kurdish refugee who came to England in 2001 after he was repeatedly jailed and tortured for his writings which criticised the Iranian regime. He left his wife and children behind in Iran and can only communicate with them via phone messages passed on by relatives. He was granted asylum in Britain, but then found out in May 2003 that the government was trying to overturn that decision and make him leave so he took drastic action. He sewed together his lips, eyelids and ears in protest. He was willing to face death if necessary in order to bring attention to the plight of refugees around the world.

For the first few days he swore his friends to secrecy about his actions, but as news leaked out about his protest he became an international cause célèbre. After 11 days he abandoned his protest and allowed a nurse to cut the threads at his eyes, mouth and ears. He said that he accepted there were other ways to fight for the rights of asylum seekers worldwide. A subsequent tribunal ruled that he was allowed to stay in this country.

Source: The Guardian, 21 May 2003

● What's your reaction to Abas Amini's action? How does it make you feel?

● How do you think the people in government who were trying to make him leave the country would have felt when they heard about his action? Would they be more sympathetic to him? Or would they be more determined to see him go?

- How does this protest compare to what happens when we fast? What are the similarities and what are the differences?

- Have you ever fasted? How did it make you feel? Did it change you in any way?

ON THE CDROM

- Fasting sheet one – Bible passages on fasting

- Fasting sheet two – comment cards outlining motives for fasting

- Fasting sheet three – outlines of the body to draw clothes on – one male and one female

GET READY

- Do you know what your denomination thinks about fasting? If you need advice on how to talk about this with your group, ask your church leader for some help.

- Be aware of any problems with eating disorders in the group, or conditions such as diabetes. Remind people that fasting doesn't have to be about giving up food – they can give up other things.

- Make one copy of Fasting sheet one and cut it into strips. Make one copy of Fasting sheet two and cut it into strips. Make enough copies of the male and female outlines on Fasting sheet three for everyone in your group to have one.

- You'll need the letters from the previous weeks plus some new envelopes.

- You will also need a flip chart and pens, Bibles, a CD player and CD and coloured pens.

READY-TO-USE GUIDE

AIM: *to introduce young people to fasting, or help them rediscover it, as an important part of our secret spirituality*

I'M A CASTAWAY SURVIVOR – GET ME OUT OF HERE!

Brainstorm a list of things that the group just can't live without. What are the gadgets, habits and tastes that are essential to your sense of well being – mobile phones, make-up, PlayStation/Gamecube, TV, Internet, cigarettes, chocolate? We're not talking about people here – just the things that are so much a part of our everyday existence that we can't imagine life without them. Compile a list on a flip chart.

Now tell the group that they have been selected for a new Reality TV show called *I'm a castaway survivor – get me out of here!* They will be marooned on a Scottish island and they will only be able to take five of these essentials with them. Which five will it be? Ask every one to vote for their top three things. Give three points for every first choice, two for every second and one for every third. Add up the points and work out which five things are most important to the group. Reassure them that it's only a game!

WHEN YOU FAST

Ask someone to read Matthew 6:16-18. If you have done the Giving and Forgiveness sessions, see if they can remember which words Jesus uses about all three activities.

● Jesus says 'when' you give, pray which includes forgiving, fast – not 'if'.

● Don't be hypocritical or a show-off.

● If you do it to be seen by other people that's all the reward you'll get.

● Giving, forgiving and fasting should be done secretly.

● God will see you and reward you.

Fasting was a normal part of Jewish life and Jesus wanted to make sure that they weren't doing it for the wrong reasons. Fasting is still emphasised in some parts of the church, but by and large it's not often talked about. Today, you'll investigate it further.

FASTING IN THE BIBLE

Split the group into four and give them each a Bible passage to investigate from the sheet on the CDROM. Select the most appropriate passage for the reading ability of the group. You may need to fill in some of the background to the stories. The four stories are:

17

- Nehemiah – chapter 1:1-2, 9

- Esther – chapter 3:5-11; 4:1-17; 7:1-10

- Jonah – chapter 3:1-10

- Barnabas and Saul – Acts 13:1-5; 14:21-25.

Get each small group to report back to the rest and discuss what they found. The Old Testament stories about fasting were serious situations. Fasting showed their strength of feeling and their desire for God to intervene. They were aware of a sense of battle and needing to fight. The New Testament examples come before making an important decision.

RIGHT MOTIVES

Jesus talks about the importance of having right motives when fasting. Hand round the comment cards from the CDROM, and discuss whether these people have got things right. How would they respond to the arguments on the cards? Suggested responses are given here:

- Joe has rather missed the point – fasting is choosing to go without food to focus on God and prayer, not seeing what you can get away with.

- Kate's motive is not a great one. Fasting is about drawing close to God, not to your ideal figure. This isn't a sensible or lasting way to lose weight anyway.

- Doug needs to realise that fasting bears fruit if it's accompanied by prayer. The idea is to invest the time you free up by not eating in praying. If you're worried about being too hungry, start small. Just miss one meal and pray instead.

- Belinda should remember that fasting doesn't change God, it changes us. We can't spiritually blackmail God into answering our prayers by fasting, but fasting does enable us to draw close to God and so hear him better. Fasting may help Belinda realise God's love for her, help her to relate to her parents better and so on, but won't force God to act in a certain way.

SO HOW DO YOU DO IT THEN?

Ask the group how they would summarise what they know about fasting – as they begin to talk, put on some really loud music so you all have to shout to make yourself heard. Turn it down and make the point that fasting often shows up the things in our lives that are drowning out God's words to us.

Fasting can be a way of controlling the things that control us. Instead of immediately rushing to satisfy our hunger for different things, it enables us to be more controlled and have a better sense of God's priorities. Fasting in the Bible was always about giving up food, and sometimes even drink – but you can also fast from anything that you feel is too important in your life. Look back at the list of 'things that you can't live without' – maybe some people would want to fast from some of these things.

Finally if they do want to fast, give them some guidelines:

- Decide what to give up and how long to do it for.

- Be realistic – start simply.

- Stay healthy – going without drink for any length of time will make you ill. Get a doctor's advice if you are diabetic. You can always fast from something other than food, such as television or video games.

- Decide how to use the time you free up – what will you pray for?

LETTER TO MYSELF

Hand back the letters they have written in previous sessions. Provide new envelopes and more paper if needed. Ask them to reflect on what they have learned this week and write down what they want to do about it. This time when they seal their letters in the envelopes, ask them to write their name and address on the front. Tell them you will post the letters to them in a month to remind them of what they decided.

DOES IT FIT?

We've looked at the importance of giving, forgiveness and fasting – of having a secret spirituality that helps us to truly worship God. Hand out copies of the Does it fit? outline from the CDROM. Our spirituality is the way we live out lives as Christians including the means of prayer, study and worship that we use to draw close to God. Like our clothes, we need to find a style that suits us and is meaningful, not feel that we are being forced to wear someone else's.

Ask the group to reflect on what they have learned about giving, forgiveness and fasting. What do they feel like: old-fashioned clothes that are embarrassing to wear? Someone else's clothes that don't really fit? A new style that they would like to get used to? Something comfortable that they will use a lot, like a favourite pair of jeans? Completely weird, like wearing an alien costume?

Suggest that they draw and write on the outlines the clothes that these disciplines suggest to them. Discuss what they have drawn and end with a time of prayer, encouraging them to voice their desires to God.

Inner Beauty

Our society is obsessed with the way people look. Magazines are full of makeovers, beauty tips, fashion spreads and diets – for men as well as women. There's nothing wrong with wanting to look good, but it's difficult not to get sucked into judging people by what they look like. God is not taken in by our outward appearance – he's more concerned about what's in our hearts. Tackle this subject with your group to remind them that they have value no matter what they look like. And that investing in their character and their relationship with God will bring more lasting rewards than hours in front of the mirror.

- Watch *Shallow Hal*, starring Gwyneth Paltrow and Jack Black. It tells the story of Hal Larsen who only dates beautiful women. After hypnosis, Hal now sees the true inner beauty of the woman in front of him. Enter Rosemary, played by Gwyneth in a 'fat suit', who in reality is overweight. Because she's such a nice person inside, Hal sees her as slim and beautiful and falls in love. When the hypnosis is broken, he's confronted with the real Rosemary and learns some important lessons. Not the best film ever, and with lots of cheap laughs, but it raises interesting questions about why we consider looks so important.

- Try going out without putting on your make-up/doing your hair/with egg stains on your jumper. (After all this is what you are going to ask some of your group to do!) Does it affect how you feel? Or how you relate to other people? How important are your looks to you? How much time do you spend on your appearance compared to how much time you spend with God – and is it appropriate to compare the two?

Some Bible passages:

Isaiah 53:1-12 *What do you think Jesus looked like? What attracted people to him?*

Esther 2:1-18 *The Bible is not anti-beauty – after all Esther is probably the most famous winner of a beauty contest. But what inner qualities did she also need in order to save her people?*

1 Peter 3:3-4 *But is there a danger that we take these words too literally and end up frumpy and old before our time? How can you get a good balance between your inner character and your outer looks?*

Discussion starter You've probably heard the phrase 'born with a silver spoon in her mouth' – used to describe someone who is born into a wealthy and privileged family. Well, Jade Jagger was born with a whole canteen of silver cutlery in hers. Her parents are Mick and Bianca Jagger and as you might expect, Jade herself is beautiful, rich and successful. She has just been made creative director of a Bond Street jewellers so she is not just a pretty face. But does her perfection go more than skin-deep?

Jade has two fantastic houses, one in Ibiza and one in London, two beautiful daughters and one very handsome boyfriend, Dan Williams. And she insists that the people who work for her look good too. 'Wow, what gorgeous staff I have,' she says, looking at one of her workmen with his top off. 'I just can't understand people who have ugly people working for them. I really can't.'

Source: The Week, 7 September 2002

● How would you reply to Jade Jagger?

● What do her words suggest about her attitudes to other people? How important are looks to you? Is it wrong to appreciate beautiful people?

● Do you think society is too obsessed with the way people look? What are the pros and cons of looking good?

● Think about your friends – what aspects of their characters make them beautiful people on the inside, regardless of what they look like? How can people develop those characteristics?

ON THE CDROM

● Inner beauty sheet one – outlines of a person, one male, one female

GET READY

- Ask a couple of group members to go to school one day or to attend this session without bothering about doing their hair or wearing make up, with holes in their socks and with breakfast down their jumpers.

- Decide which icebreaker will work with your group. For the sophisticated option you will need pictures of lots of different types of people. For the gross option you will need ginger biscuits, orange juice, sweetcorn, chocolate sauce, a liquidizer, some kitchen roll and two pound coins. Arrange this on a piece of clingfilm on a table or a chopping board so it is easy to clear up!

- Think through what inner blemishes you want to confess to in 'making it visible' and collect the things you need.

- Make copies of Inner beauty sheet one, enough for the boys and girls in your group.

- Empty the beauty contents of your bathroom cabinet to use as parallels for spiritual disciplines.

- You will also need some passion fruit, kiwi fruit, pens, a sharp knife and some plates.

READY-TO-USE GUIDE

AIM: *to show the importance of 'Inner Beauty' to God, to consider how beautiful they are 'inside' and to show how to develop and maintain their inner selves.*

ICEBREAKER

Try either or both of these to introduce the subject.

a) The sophisticated option.

Collect pictures of a wide variety of people, celebrities and ordinary, gorgeous and run-of-the-mill. Stick these up around the room and ask your group to judge who is the most beautiful. You are asking them to judge on outward appearances here, but see if there is any mention of how 'beautiful' the life style or character of the person in the picture is. Introduce this idea in discussion afterwards if it hasn't come up. Would that affect who gets chosen as most beautiful person? Point out that many people who we consider stunningly beautiful often express dissatisfaction with the way they appear.

b) The gross option.

Soak ginger biscuits in orange juice and liquidize. Add some sweet corn and streaks of chocolate sauce. Hide a couple of pound coins in there and arrange on a tray in a cow-pat shape! You could invent some really gross story about how you lost some money in a field and a cow happened to be passing.... Tell them they can have the money IF they fish it out with their teeth – no hands allowed. (Be nice and have kitchen roll ready for those brave enough to try it!)

Read Proverbs 11:22. Pigs were unclean animals to the Jews so the idea of a gold ring in a pig's nose was outrageous – completely out of place and inappropriate. Icebreaker b) is a modern equivalent – money in a cowpat. The writer likens that to a beautiful person who acts unwisely, someone whose character lets them down, someone who looks good on the outside but has no inner beauty to match. What's more, the lack of inner beauty completely overshadows any outer beauty. A Jew seeing the pig would think 'how disgusting', not 'what a beautiful gold ring'.

DISCUSSION ONE

Ask how your 'ungroomed' guinea pigs got on at school, or coming to the group? Did the fact they were less well presented outwardly affect how they felt about themselves? How did other people react to them? Ask other members of the group how they feel on a 'bad-hair day'. Often, knowing we look good increases our confidence, which is why we spend time on our appearance. Does the state of our 'inner beauty' affect us in the same way? Why?

MAKING IT VISIBLE

Talk about the state of your inner self, and translate any inner blemishes into visible ones. For example, 'I argued with my brother and still haven't resolved it' could be represented by a big felt-penned zit on the end of your nose. 'I gossiped about a friend this week' could be the inner equivalent of greasy hair – plaster hair gel on to get the effect. 'I'm really envious of my friend's new car' could be shown by smearing chocolate down your front. Don't make yourself more vulnerable than you feel comfortable with, but bear in mind that you are about to ask them to do the same exercise themselves, although they will be doing it privately.

Give group members copies of the Inner Beauty sheet and access to pens. Ask them to do what you have just done – think about the state of their inner selves and draw or write on the figures on the sheet how these inner blemishes might appear if they were visible. Allow them some privacy – this is between them and God.

Draw this activity to a close by reminding them that if our inner blemishes were this visible we might make more effort to address them. But when we come before God, he effectively turns us inside out – these are the things he sees and we can't hide them.

BIBLE ILLUSTRATION

Get a group member to tell or read the story of Samuel going to Jesse's family to choose the next King of Israel (1 Sam. 16:1-13). The key verse is 7 – 'people look at the outward appearance but the Lord looks at the heart.' David wasn't even included in the line-up of the brothers because his family considered him so inappropriate to be king. His brothers all looked very impressive outwardly but that was not what God was after. David was actually very good looking himself, but what was important to God was the state of his heart.

DISCUSSION TWO

What characteristics make someone beautiful inside? Get them to think of people they know who have true inner beauty – what are they like? Expect mentions of the fruit of the spirit, wisdom, generosity, humility. Write these up so they can be seen. How much do they want to be like that?

THE INNER BEAUTY ROUTINE

Ask what they use to make themselves presentable on the outside and bring examples of what you think they might say – shower gel, shampoo, deodorant, toothpaste, make-up, hair spray. Point out that it is only Jesus who can transform us from the inside, but we can do a lot to co-operate with that. With the contents of your bathroom and the list of aspects of inner beauty in front of them, can they think of spiritual equivalents that will improve their Inner Beauty? Look for things like spending time with God, resolving arguments quickly, asking for and extending forgiveness, reading about Jesus, worshipping, having accountability, taking advice, spending time with God's people. How could they better include some of these things in their daily routine?

PASSION FRUIT

Pass round passion fruit or kiwi fruit. Both have unattractive outsides – either black and wrinkled or hairy – but delicious insides. Encourage them to eat some of the fruit as a way of saying to God that they want to be beautiful inside. Give them some space to bring to God the inner blemishes they drew on their sheets earlier. Pray for them, that the Holy Spirit will transform them from within and that they will co-operate with that.

God with us

One of the names that Jesus was given before his birth was Emmanuel, God with us. So this session would fit well at Christmas time but you could of course do it at any time of the year.

● The beginning of the film *The Miracle Maker* shows Jesus working in his home village. The first six and a half minutes give glimpses of what Jesus might have done before he started his ministry; working as a carpenter, talking to his mother, choosing to leave his trade in order to do his Father's work. The clip ends with Mary sitting beside Jesus' bed with the gifts from the wise men to show him and brings home the fact that Jesus was fully human like us.

● Some young people may be a bit spooked out by the thought that God is always there, looking at them, like a celestial version of *Big Brother*. Check out the *Big Brother* website on www.channel4.com and think about how you might address this one. Lots of *Big Brother* contestants are very aware of the cameras and play up accordingly. Should the fact that God can see everything we do affect our behaviour? If so, how?

● Avril Lavigne's song *I'm with you* on her album *Let Go* talks about standing in the cold and dark, waiting and longing for someone to take her home. She sings 'Won't you take me by the hand take me somewhere new; I don't know who you are but I'm with you.' You could use this song in worship, asking young people to listen to the words and reflect on the times when God has drawn close to them when they have been most needy. Can they respond by saying 'I'm with you' to God?

Some Bible passages:

John 1:10-14 *What must it have been like for Jesus to be in the world among the people that he created and yet to get such a mixed reaction from them?*

John 14:15-21 *Jesus' beautiful promise to not leave us as orphans.*

Matthew 28:19,20 *Jesus gives his disciples an awesome task, but promises to be with them. Has this been true in your life?*

▶▶ Discussion starter Show a clip from the film *The Truman Show* (cert PG). Truman Burbank, played by Jim Carrey, has lived in the town of Seahaven all his life. But unbeknown to him, he is the central character in a reality TV show; every minute of his life is being transmitted and watched by people around the globe. He was even born on TV and since then Christof, the director of the TV programme, has controlled his life. Truman's friends and family are all actors; the products he uses are all opportunities for advertisements. During the film, he becomes aware of the truth about his life when he hears Christof's voice on the radio and sees a light fall from the sky. He disappears one day, no mean feat when you consider that there are always cameras on him, and Christof and the production team organise all the actors to search for him. This clip starts with Christof desperate to find him, ordering the sun to be turned on even though it's still night time. He discovers that Truman has got into a boat and is trying to escape across the sea. Christof orders a storm over the sea to try and get Truman to turn back. Truman reaches the edge of the set, and then Christof speaks to him appealing to him to stay. The clip starts just after the search reaches the bridge and someone calls for more batteries. The clip ends after Truman says 'In case I don't see you, good afternoon, good evening and good night' and walks through the door marked exit. You'll be asking the group to contrast Christof with God; what are the differences between the Creator of the universe and the creator of *The Truman Show*; you may want to alert them to this before showing the clip.

Clip start time: 1:16:30
Clip end time: 1:31:20
Length of clip: nearly 15 minutes

DISCUSS WITH THE GROUP:

● Christof is the creator of *The Truman Show*; God is the Creator of the universe. Can you see any similarities between them? How is Christof a bit like God?

- What are the differences between Christof and God?

- Christof says that he has been watching Truman since he was born and that he knows Truman better than Truman knows himself. Do you agree with this?

- God doesn't just watch us from afar. What has he done that is better? (see Jn. 1:14 and Heb. 2:14-18)

- What difference does it make to your life, knowing that Jesus has lived on earth as a human being?

ON THE CDROM

- God with us sheet one – tracing Jesus' journey from heaven to us

GET READY

- If you are not doing this at Christmas, remove any references to it from the notes below!

- Find some objects to provide smells, sounds and touches for the Sensory overload game. I suggested a cut lemon, a bowl of fresh ground coffee, a jar of marmite, a small bell, a crinkly crisp packet, coins to jingle, a feather, a pebble and a silk scarf. You'll also need a scarf for a blindfold.

- Collect together the objects to teach how God is with us today – a football chart song or football scarves, ink pads and paper, nightlights and matches.

- Make copies of God with us sheet one from the CDROM – enough for one each.

- You will also need red nail varnish, pens and Bibles.

READY-TO-USE GUIDE

AIM: *to explore the meaning of one of the names used to foretell Jesus' birth – Emmanuel – and to consider how he is with us today.*

SENSORY OVERLOAD

Can you detect who someone is by their smell/touch/sound? To play this game, your group sits in a circle with a blindfolded member at the centre – the sensor. You provide smells (a cut lemon, a bowl of fresh ground coffee, a jar of marmite), sounds (a small bell, a crinkly crisp packet, coins to jingle) and touchy things (a feather, a pebble, a silk scarf.) Once the sensor is blindfolded, everyone else chooses an object and sits in a different place in the circle. In turn, people call out their name and the object they have chosen. Select one person to start by walking across the circle making sure the sensor hears, smells, or touches their object. They swap places with someone else who then walks across the circle. The sensor has to call out the name of each person that goes past them using their senses and memory. Make a note of how many people they correctly identify. When everyone has moved, let the sensor know how many he or she got right. Choose a new sensor and get everyone to swap objects – it gets more difficult the more times you play.

GOD AWARE

Christmas is a time to celebrate the incarnation of Jesus – the fact that he left his home with God and came to spend time on earth as a human. And yet it is very easy to let Christmas celebrations crowd Jesus out. Ask the group: When have they been most aware of God at Christmas? What about the rest of their lives – how aware are they from day to day that God is with them? What helps or hinders being aware of his presence? Broaden the discussion to think about times when friends and family have supported them and made a difference by being there for them. How have they in turn supported others?

Usually we use our senses to detect whether someone is physically with us (refer back to the game) – we can see them for a start! God can't be seen, smelt or touched but that doesn't mean that he is not there – we need to learn different ways of being aware of the fact that he is Emmanuel – God with us.

BIBLE STUDY – JESUS' JOURNEY

Hand out copies of the Jesus' journey sheet from the CDROM and make sure everyone has pens and Bibles. The Bible passages on the sheet talk about the journey Jesus took from being with God at creation, through spending time here on earth, to returning to God and yet remaining with us by his spirit. Get group members to look up the passages and summarise what each one is about in the circle next to it.

1) John 1:1-2 At creation, Jesus is with God.

2) Isaiah 7:14 Jesus birth is foretold and he is given the name Emmanuel

3) Matthew 1:18-23 Mary conceives Jesus, and again he is called Emmanuel

4) Matthew 4:18-22 First disciples follow Jesus

5) Matthew 10:1-7 Jesus gives the disciples authority and sends them out – to do things without him physically there

6) John 14:15-20 Jesus talks about leaving but remaining with them

7) Matthew 28:16-20 Jesus passes on the Great Commission, and promises to remain with them

8) Acts 2:1-4, 37-41 The Holy Spirit comes and people are saved.

BUT HOW IS HE 'WITH US'?

Use the following objects to teach in what ways God is with us now. You could introduce the object and see if they can make the connections themselves. You could hand out Christmas cards and get them to write down the Bible references inside to look up and read once they are at home.

A SUPPORTER – EPHESIANS 3:17-19

Play a football chart song or hand out some football scarves and get them to make up chants. Football fans often talk about their team as if they were actually a part of it. 'We're with you all the way'; 'We're on our way to the cup' – when in fact they are just going to watch a match on the TV.

God is with us in the sense that he loves us, supports us, wants to see us grow and flourish, has fought for us and thinks we are great!

INCARNATE – HEBREWS 2:14-18

Ask group members to swap shoes with someone next to them and walk around in them – how does it feel? Try another pair, perhaps someone with quite different size feet.

God is with us because he has experienced what it is like to live here on earth as a human. Jesus felt the same things that we do, he can empathise with us and understand the difficulties we face. He chose to

31

walk in our shoes, a totally different experience to his life with God in heaven. For him, that led to suffering and death, but he did it for us.

VISIBLE IN CREATION – ROMANS 1:18-20

Pass round a couple of inkpads and some paper. Get group members to make a picture of a tree or flower with their fingerprints.

God has left his fingerprints all over creation. The intricacy of the natural world, and the beauty and wonder of the way God has made us point to who he is and what he is like. Have they ever been aware of God when watching a beautiful sunset or walking along the beach? That's because these things are signposts to the God who created everything and keeps it all going.

INDWELLING – JOHN 14:16-17

Sit in a circle and give everyone a nightlight. Light your nightlight and allow the person next to you to light theirs from yours. Pass the flame around the circle until all are lit.

When Jesus returned to God, he promised that he would leave his Spirit behind with his disciples. This happened dramatically at Pentecost and happens each time someone commits their life to Jesus – the flame of God's Spirit is lit in their life and he lives in us.

WITH GOD, WITHOUT GOD

Remind the group of the Weetabix withabix/withoutabix advertising campaign. There's a copy of the Black Beauty ad on their website www.weetabix.co.uk. Does Weetabix really make this much difference?!

Write 'With God' on one sheet of paper and 'Without God' on another. Get your group to write down in their own words the difference that Emmanuel, God with us, makes to their lives.

REMEMBER, REMEMBER

To help them remember that God is with them this coming Christmas, or through the coming week, hand round some red nail varnish and get them to paint one fingernail a Christmassy red. Every time they look at it, they can thank God that he is with them.

Seasons

When someone first becomes a Christian, they are often amazingly aware of God's love, of how much they have been forgiven and how much they owe to Jesus. Prayer and reading the Bible are exciting, not a chore. And then as time goes on, that changes. Not because they love God any less, but because it's just not possible to live on that high all the time. Dealing with that change in feelings can be difficult. People can wonder whether they have done something wrong, or whether God loves them less. In fact, it's just part of the rhythm of life. Just as nature goes through cycles of winter, spring, summer and autumn, so we will go through that same pattern in our relationship with God; sometimes it feel like summer, when everything is sweet and life is fruitful. At other times it will feel like winter when everything is dead, and hope is gone. But the thing to remember in the deepest, coldest winter is that spring always comes.

- The theme of seasons inevitably brings to mind countryside and trees. It's a myth that it's easier to find God surrounded by fields and empty spaces and it's important that young people are able to find ways to relate to God in the places where they live. When you find a tree to look at for this session, it doesn't matter if it's surrounded by concrete and buildings – it's still a tree, changing through the seasons in the place where it's rooted. Vaux is an alternative worship group in London exploring urban spirituality and what it means to follow Christ in an urban context. They have some interesting material on their site www.vaux.net/archive – in particular sections 26 to 28 which are liturgies for the city and section 31, an urban mass.

- This guide asks group members to think back over the last year to see if they can identify times when they felt close to God and times when they felt further away; it will help if you do the exercise with them and talk about how your year has gone. Can you identify with this theme of seasons? When did you last go through an autumnal time, when it felt as though everything was dying? Can you remember what it was like to experience spring in your relationship with God – a time of hope and new life after a long period of distance?

Some Bible passages:

Genesis 8:22 *God's promise to Noah about the seasons; is it fair to say that this applies to our spiritual lives too?*

Romans 8:35-39 *What can separate us from the love of Christ?*

Psalm 40:1-3 *The psalm that has been sung by thousands in rock concerts thanks to U2; perhaps an example of winter to spring?*

Galatians 5:22,23 *How will the fruit of the Spirit help us cope with seasons in our relationship with God?*

Discussion starter Play the track *Bring me to life* from the album *Fallen* by Evanescence (2003 Wind Up records) The lyrics to the song can be found at www.azlyrics.com/lyrics/evanescence/bringmetolife.html and the band's website is at www.evanecence.com. This track was at number 1 in the UK charts for 4 weeks in 2003. Their blend of Gothic rock with haunting lyrics by Amy Lee has made a huge impact on this side of the Atlantic. Their debut single was met with lots of discussion about their Christian faith or lack of it. Suffice it to say that some of the band are Christians, and you can see the influence of faith on some of their lyrics, but not all of them are and perhaps like U2, they prefer not to be pigeonholed as a Christian band.

● This song describes how numb someone feels after breaking up with their partner. Are there any situations that might make someone feel like this about their relationship with God? What might they be?

● Ask someone from the group to read Psalm 13. Who was it written by? David is one of the key figures of the Bible, known for defeating Goliath and being a strong king. And yet here, he is in despair, feeling far from God. Why do people go through times like this?

● The song says 'wake me up inside; save me from the nothing I've become.' What can you do if you feel like this spiritually?

- Have you ever experienced a time when God seemed far away? Did anything happen to spark it off? How did things change?

- Explain the concept of seasons in our spiritual lives, using the notes in the ready-to-use guide below. Does that idea make sense? Is it helpful? Can you identify times when you have been in different 'seasons'?

- This song, if sung by someone to God, would describe someone experiencing winter. What would you say to them to give them hope? Invite the group to write a verse of the song, expressing the certainty that spring is coming.

ON THE CDROM

- Seasons sheet one – a list of dates to adapt for the quiz

- Seasons sheet two – a chart to do a review of the year

- Seasons sheet three – Bible passages for your group to look up

GET READY

- You will need access to a tree – ideally one close to where you meet so that the group can go and stand round it during and at the end of the session. If there are no trees near enough to walk to or if it is pouring with rain, you may be able to see one out of the window of the place where you meet. Failing that, take some photos of a tree or get hold of a picture of a tree showing it during the season in which you are meeting.

- Seasons sheet one contains the names of some festivals and their dates. Add the correct dates for the festivals given – to make it harder just give the number of the day and not the month. You'll split your group into teams of three or four to play the game. Make a copy for each team and cut them into sets of cards – make sure you shuffle each set before you hand them out.

- Make copies of seasons sheet two, enough for your group to have one each. Make one copy of seasons sheet three and cut it into sections.

- You'll also need pens, a CD player and chillout music, a gold pen and Bibles.

AIM: *to explore how we can live in the rhythm of God's seasons.*

THE DATING GAME

Split your group into teams and give each a set of festivals and a set of dates from the CDROM. The first team to match up the festivals and dates and place them in the correct order through the year is the winner.

Answers:

New Year's Day – 1 January

Valentine's Day – 14 February

Shrove Tuesday – depends on the year

Good Friday – depends on the year

May Day bank holiday – first Monday in May

Father's Day – usually third Sunday in June

All Saints Day – 1 November

1st Sunday in Advent – four Sundays before Christmas

Boxing Day – 26 December

Youth leader's birthday – add the correct date!

REVIEW OF THE YEAR

Looking back over the last year, you can probably remember what you were doing and how you felt on each of these festivals, but how has the last year been for you in your spiritual life? Hand out copies of the Review of the year sheet from the CDROM. Give them space to think about what they have experienced in the last year and how they have felt in their relationship with God. They may find it easier to write down events that have happened and then draw the ups and downs of the year. Play some music in the background. Once the charts are drawn ask people to reflect for a moment on the ups and downs. What happened just before each significant up or down? Can you identify a cause for each up or down? Before they go too far down this road, talk about your chart. Sometimes, we choose to disobey God or 'step back' in our relationship with him, and consequently we don't feel so close. At other times there is no reason why we feel close to God or further away and looking for a reason can be counter-productive – it leads us to a 'salvation by works' syndrome, feeling that God will be pleased with us and love us if we do all the right things like read our Bibles, and he'll be unhappy if we don't. Point out on your chart the times when you can see reasons for the ups and downs, and times when you can't.

FIND A TREE

Leave all the charts behind and take the group outside to find a tree, or produce the pictures. Ask group members to imagine and discuss what the tree will look like during the seasons of the year. What is their favourite season? How do they feel looking at trees in different seasons – assuming they have noticed the changes? Get someone to read Ecclesiastes 3 v 1-8. Explain that just as trees go through seasons and change according to the time of year, so our spiritual lives go through a rhythm of seasons of the soul.

Spring – time of new growth, new beginnings;

Summer – time of plenty, feeling close to God;

Autumn – things coming to an end, preparing for change;

Winter – time of hardship/pain/loss when you don't feel very alive.

BIBLE STUDY

Back inside, have a look at how characters in the Bible experienced different seasons. Split the group into four and give each a passage and the questions to think about, using the sheet on the CDROM. (The first passage assumes the least previous Bible knowledge, the last one assumes the most.) They should spend some time reading and discussing, and then report back to the rest of the group on their character, giving reasons for their answer. The expected 'answers' for the passages are spring, winter, summer, autumn, but see if your group agree!

John 1 v 3-30, and v 39.

● What season would you say the woman was in after she met Jesus?

● What was her life like before meeting Jesus? What season might she have been in?

Ruth 1 v 1-21

● What season might Naomi have said she was in at this point in her life?

● Did life change? Look at Ruth 4 v 13-17. What season is this?

Acts 2 v 1-15, v 40-42

● What season is Peter in here?

● What else do you know about Peter's life? Can you remember stories of him in other seasons? (Have a look at John 21 v 15-19; John 6 v 60-69)

1 Kings 18 v 1-39 and 19 v 1-18

What season was Elijah in during chapter 19? Is this what you expect – he's just had a great triumph in chapter 18.

Finish this section by reminding the group of the importance of seasons in the natural world. Winter may be a time when everything seems to be dead, but it is also a time of preparation for the spring when things come to life again. Hot summers are great, but the land needs the rains of autumn, and the richness that the dead leaves bring to the soil. Recognising the same seasons in our spiritual lives can be liberating – instead of blaming ourselves if we are in an autumn or winter phase, we can stay faithful and learn to wait and see what God is doing.

WHAT SEASON ARE YOU IN?

Get the group to look at their charts again and think about what season they feel they are in. Invite them to draw a picture of a tree in this season in the corner of their chart. As they do this, go round to them one by one and draw a line in gold across the top of their chart labelled 'How God feels about you'. Whatever season they are in, God's love remains constant, whether they feel it or not. If you think your group are up for it, discuss the drawings. Get group members to talk about how they feel and share any specific prayer requests.

BACK TO THE TREE

Go back outside again and stand round the tree. Read Genesis 8:22. This was God's promise to Noah that as long as the earth endures, the seasons will follow each other. For those who feel they are in a time of winter, spring is coming. For those who feel they are in a summer phase, autumn will come, but is not to be feared. Finish with a time of prayer around the tree, praying for individuals if they have talked about their pictures, or more generally if they have not. Encourage those who feel springlike or summery to support and encourage those who face autumn or winter.

Engaging with the Bible

This session would be a good introduction to a longer series giving an overview of the Bible. This is for use with young people who struggle with Bible reading, but don't assume that all young people do! Find out if it is an issue for your group.

- The version of Bible you use with young people is important, and there are several versions of youth Bibles available. Point out to young people all the additional material that comes with these Bibles – there are usually notes on how to read it, where to find different sections, background information and material that applies passages to issues that young people face. There's no shame in using the contents page to find your way round the Bible – make sure they know that.

- An inclusive language version such as the CEV, NCV or TNIV will make sure verses don't jar with their awareness of gender issues. The Bible Gateway website has sixteen different versions of the Bible including The Message that you can access and print off – www.Bible.gospelcom.net. For people who are not used to reading the Bible, a printed sheet of the relevant verses may be more accessible than an actual Bible, but of course it doesn't help them to find their way around it.

- Questions about the authenticity and accuracy of the Bible may well come up in this session. They're not addressed here because there's not time to do everything in one session, so be prepared to come back to them. Your church leader should be able to lend you books on the background to the Bible and help you answer questions.

Some Bible passages:

James 1:16-27 *Reading it is not enough; it's what you do with what you've read that counts. When was the last time that a Bible passage affected your actions?*

2 Timothy 3:14 – 4:5 *Do you know enough of the Bible to be able to discern false teaching about it?*

Acts 8:26-40 *What do you find difficult to understand about the Bible? Who do you turn to for help?*

Discussion starter   Use a clip from the film *Waterworld* (cert 12). First, find out common perceptions of the Bible by asking the group how their friends at school view it. What words would they use to describe the Bible? People can tend to see it as out of date, irrelevant, unreliable or contradictory. And yet Christians treat the Bible as a very important book; it's God's word to us.

Explain that it can be difficult sometimes to see how the Bible connects to our everyday lives; it can seem like it belongs to a different world. Introduce a clip from the film *Waterworld*; ask them to think if they can see any connections with this clip and the Bible!

The clip comes right at the start of the film and the story is explained from the beginning. The film is set in the future when the icecaps have melted and the whole earth is covered in water. The Mariner, played by Kevin Costner, is the hero of the film, a self-sufficient drifter who has adapted to a new world. The clip starts from the Universal logo as this runs into the beginning of the film. The clip ends after the Mariner's boat has sliced off the mast of the other drifter and the Smokers attack him.

Clip start time: 0:00
Clip end time: 8:58
Length of clip: about nine minutes

Ask if anyone can see the connection between the clip and the Bible – it'll be surprising if they can, but at least you have got them thinking!

● The Mariner dives down to the old world beneath the sea to find useful items. Did you see anything on his boat that he had found and then used? (There was a harmonica, some metal bits in a wind chime, a chair, some kind of typewriter)

● Do you think the Mariner valued the 'junk' he had found? Why? (he was prepared to leave his boat to go and find it; he was prepared to risk getting nearer the Smokers to grab the bag of stuff he had found.)

- In this totally new submerged world, things from the past still had value. Why do you think that is?

Point out the connection with the Bible; although our world is very different to the time that the Bible was written, there are still treasures to be found in it that are very useful and relevant to today. In fact the more the world changes, the more people want wisdom and truth that has stood the test of time. Although God still speaks to people today, the wisdom contained in the Bible still stands the test of time. People who live by it find abundant life in God. Many of the values and principles that inform their decisions will have come from the Bible in the first place.

ON THE CDROM

- Engaging with the Bible sheet one – suggestions for different passages to read in the Bible

GET READY

- Make copies of Engaging with the Bible sheet one, enough for everyone to have one of the slips; you may want to adapt or repeat some of them.

- Before the group arrive, set out lots of different things that they can read – books, newspapers, different sorts of magazines, comics, a couple of different editions of the Bible, an envelope with their name on containing a letter to them, a computer with Internet access if possible, brochures for a holiday or theme park and so on.

- Read 'The Bible is like...' section and decide which objects you want to use as metaphors for the Bible. I've suggested the highway code, an encyclopaedia, a novel, a history text book, a child's story book, a vitamin pill, a puzzle book, a mirror, clothes, an autobiography, a website and some trainers.

- You will need a flip chart and pens and Bibles.

READY-TO-USE GUIDE

AIM: *to explore honestly the difficulties that young people have with the Bible*

to suggest some creative ways of engaging with the Bible.

INTRODUCTION

As the group members arrive, explain that you're a bit behind and you'd really appreciate it if they found something to read for ten minutes. At the end of ten minutes gather them all together and find out:

● What did you choose to read and why?

● How much do you read for pleasure? What kind of things do you choose to read? What was the last thing you read that really inspired you?

● How much do you read because you have to?

● What have you read in the last week?

● Did anyone choose to read the Bible just now? Why or why not?

BRAINSTORM

Expand the last question from the introduction to explore the reasons why people struggle with Bible reading. Use a flip chart and tell them that this is a Total Honesty Zone. They probably all feel that they ought to read the Bible. What are some of the reasons why they don't read the Bible? Record their answers on the flip chart, and allow them to offload all their negativity about Bible reading. Do these reasons come from having read the Bible and been put off, or have they never really got into it?

Then ask: So, shall we just ignore it, then, if it's so difficult to get into? Ask them to list all the reasons why they think Bible reading is important – it could be things that other people have told them, or their own beliefs. Record these on a fresh sheet of the flip chart. If you have a group of mainly unchurched young people or young Christians, they may not come up with many reasons. Be ready to produce reasons that you have heard other people say for their consideration.

Finally get the group to vote for how convincing they find these reasons. For each reason, get the group to imagine a line across the room, with one end representing totally convincing and the other representing totally unconvincing. Ask them to stand at the place on the line that corresponds with their view. Ask some of them why they have chosen that place. You may like to ban the words 'should' and 'ought' for this bit! Which are the three most convincing reasons? Be prepared to give your view. Discuss what has helped them read the Bible in the past and add suggestions of your own or that you have gained from other people if they don't have much to contribute.

THE BIBLE IS LIKE...

How should we treat the Bible? What kind of book is it? Find examples of the things in the following list to show some common ways the Bible has been viewed. Hold them up and ask the group to guess the link with the Bible. Is this a helpful way of viewing the Bible or not?

- Highway code – a rulebook that tells you how to live your life. Whatever you need advice on, there's a verse somewhere that will apply.

- Encyclopaedia – a source of facts

- Novel – a story book to be read from start to finish

- History text book – facts from the past to be learned

- Child's story book – a simple, easy-to-understand book.

- Vitamin pill – something that's good for you that you should take daily

There is some truth in some of these metaphors, but none of them are sufficient ways of viewing the Bible on their own. The fact is that the Bible is a book like no other. Here are some other ways to view the Bible – again ask them to guess the connection:

- A puzzle book – full of questions as much as answers. The Bible needs to be engaged with and thought about – it's not easy!

- A mirror – when we read the Bible we see ourselves reflected in the stories – how does this apply to me? How does it show me what I am like?

- Clothes – we can choose whether we are going to 'wear' the Bible or not – is it going to go beyond head knowledge to affect the way we live our lives?

- Autobiography – in that it tells us what God is like – it's a way of finding out more about him

- Trainers – anyone wanting to get fit has to exercise and it's not always inspiring. With their eyes on the bigger goal of completing a race or event, the exercise is worthwhile.

- A website – full of lots of things that can spark our interest and set us off on journeys of discovery.

You can add other ideas of your own. Ask if any of these ideas are helpful. Use the last example, the website, to point out that to get the most out of the Bible we need to have a connection to God, to expect to meet him through the pages of the Bible.

TRY THIS AT HOME

The sheet on the CDROM has suggestions for different passages to read in the Bible and different approaches. Add other ideas, adapt or repeat some to make sure that there are enough for each member of the group. Put the slips in a hat and ask everybody to draw out one. Encourage them to engage with the Bible during the week in the way described on the paper – if they want to! The following week you could find out what has worked for them and swap the ideas. Be prepared to lend people Bibles if necessary, or a concordance. If there's time in the session you could try one of these ideas altogether.

- Read the book of Ruth all the way through in one sitting. How would you summarise God's role in the story?

- Read several different versions of Ephesians 3 v 14-21. Which do you find easiest to relate to and why?

- Rewrite Romans 8 v 28-39 in your own words, using things that are relevant to you.

- Write each verse of Psalm 103 v 1-14 on a different Post-it note and stick them round your bedroom so that you read them several times a day.

- Find an intriguing story – try Judges 3 v 12-30. Ask other members of your youth group for other ideas of unknown stories to read.

- What does the Bible say about anger? Is it different in the Old and New Testaments? Use a concordance or ask other Christians for verses that they know.

- Read John 13 v 1-17 every day for a week. Ask God to speak to you through it.

- Read Matthew 5 v 38-48. What if you took this really seriously and did what it said – how would it affect your life? What would need to change?

- Read John 8 v 1-11 through several times slowly. Imagine you are one of the people in the story. What do you see, think, feel, hear? What does Jesus say to you?

Creativity

What is it that makes some people creative, able to come up with new ideas and ways of doing things? Is it a natural ability or something they have learned? If you haven't got it, is there any way of developing it? Edward de Bono, a pioneer in thinking skills, argues that there is. He believes that creative thinking is something that can be learned and in his book, *Teach your child to think*, says 'The... reason why we have neglected creative thinking ... is that we have believed that nothing can be done about it. We have considered creative thinking to be a mystical gift that some people have and others do not have. There is nothing that can be done except to foster the creative gift in those who seem to have it.' He then goes on to explain specific thinking skills that can help people to be creative. This session aims to do the same thing, unlocking precious creativity in your group!

- As you'll see below, one of the biggest blocks to creativity is the 'this is how it's done' attitude and is there any area of life where that is more prevalent than in the church? As well as talking to your group about creativity, you may need to talk to your church leadership too. But don't try to change central church services straight away; that may be too threatening. What you need is a space on the edge of things where you are free to experiment and be creative. From there your influence will spread.

- James Dyson is perhaps Britain's best-known inventor. One of his first inventions was a wheelbarrow with a ball instead of a wheel. Creator of the first bagless vacuum cleaner, he completely transformed the experience and look of household cleaning. He developed it in his back garden and had to borrow £1 million to launch it himself when he failed to get interest from any investors. He has since invented a washing machine with two drums that rotate in opposite directions. His latest development is a vacuum cleaner that can tell you when it needs to be repaired. He has also created a fountain that appears to have water flowing uphill based on Escher's

47

drawings. Sadly, his robot vacuum cleaner that will do the cleaning for you is taking longer to develop than he had hoped.

Source: The Observer, 5 November 2000

Some Bible passages:

Genesis 1:1-31 *God, of course, is the original Creator, filling the earth with amazing diversity, complexity, order and chaos. Is it any wonder that, being made in his image, we have echoes of that creativeness too?*

Romans 1:20 *God's fingerprints are all over the world, giving clues to who he is so there's no excuse not to know him.*

Exodus 31:1-5 *One of my favourite passages – here is someone anointed with the Spirit to be creative. Who might God be anointing in your group for that same purpose?*

Discussion starter Show a clip from the film *Pleasantville* (cert 12). David Wagner, played by Toby Maguire, is a teenager obsessed with a 1950s black and white sitcom called Pleasantville. Pleasantville is a perfect town where everything happens in the same routine, there have never been any arguments, passion, art, rain or colour; books have blank pages, the school basketball team always wins and every day starts with cooked breakfast. David has an argument with his sister Jennifer, played by Reese Witherspoon, over the TV and their remote control gets broken. A strange TV repairman appears outside their house and gives them a weird replacement. When they use this to turn on the TV, they find they are suddenly transported into Pleasantville. David becomes Bud and Jennifer becomes Mary Sue. They are wearing 1950s clothes and they are both now black and white.

Jennifer as Mary Sue brings her 1990s attitudes into the blandness of Pleasantville and introduces passion and questioning into the lives of the young people. Gradually some of the people and surroundings turn into colour, and the teenagers of the town get hooked on reading, music and visiting Lover's Lane! Unsurprisingly, some of the older members of the town don't like the changes, and Big Bob, the chair of the town's chamber of commerce, calls a meeting.

Choose which clip to show. The longer one shows a painting of a naked woman which may not be appropriate for your group. It starts after David and his girlfriend talk to two boys in a car. Cue the clip after one of the boys says, 'You can come over and make oatmeal cookies for me any time.' The shorter clip starts after the café has been destroyed. In both clips we see Big Bob proposing that the townspeople issue a code of conduct to restore Pleasantville to what it was. The teenagers in the nearby diner read it in dismay, but Bud tells them that they don't have to do what it says. The clip ends when he plugs the juke box back in and plays some music.

Clip start time: 1:21:45 or 1:29:33
Clip end time: 1:32.50
Length of clip: eleven minutes or nearly four and a half minutes

DISCUSS WITH THE GROUP:

- (longer clip) What makes David's character change colour?

- (longer clip) What did the TV repairman show David that he has done wrong? What Bible story does this link to? What is the film trying to say here? Do you agree?

- Why do you think the townspeople were angry about the colour? Do you think they really preferred to live in a black and white world?

- Do you think people in our society are as resistant to change? Are there any areas of life in particular where this is true?

- What areas of life do the townspeople want to restrict in their charter? Why are they so negative about creativity?

- What stops you being creative? How can you bring more colour, passion and creativity into the world?

ON THE CDROM

- Creativity sheet one – twenty random words to spark creativity

- Creativity sheet two – twenty ways to solve a problem

GET READY

- Routine can block creativity – always doing things the same way stops us seeing new possibilities. Choose a different venue for the session – the park, your local swimming pool cafe, the fountain in the shopping arcade, an art gallery, in a lift...- and let everyone know where and when you will be meeting.

- You need to arrange for a person to be delivered to the venue tied with five strips of cloth with one of the 'blocks to creativity' below written on each of them. Be as obscure as you want to – a car could arrive driven by two people dressed as a pantomime horse who then pull the victim out of the boot, drop them and disappear.

- Ask a couple of group members to prepare the creation presentation in What does the Bible say?

- Make one copy of Creativity sheet one from the CDROM and one of Creativity sheet two. If you have a large group, you might want to split into smaller groups to do this so make enough copies of both sheets.

- You will also need flip chart and pens, a dart board and darts,

READY-TO-USE GUIDE

AIM: *to emphasise that God is in the business of creativity*
        to explore ways in which to unlock their creativity

ICEBREAKER

Show them a black dot on a white piece of paper and ask them what it is. There's something that happens between primary and secondary school with respect to creativity. Little kids will see endless possibilities – a lonely Smartie, a lost coin seen from a tall tree, a drawing pin stuck on the bottom of someone's shoe – teenagers want to find 'the right answer'. Give space for their imagination to get working. Throw in some random words and look for associations. What could this have to do with ice-cream, with perfume, basketball, a magnet, sleep...?

BLOCKS TO CREATIVITY

Arrange for your bound and gagged person to be brought in at this point. Liken the victim to your imagination. Untie the five strips of cloth one by one and explain what can stop us being creative:

The right answer – sometimes education can seem to be about playing a game of 'guess what the teacher is thinking'. We feel we must find the right answer and are afraid to get things wrong.

It won't work – as soon as we have an idea, we judge it and think of all the reasons it won't work. We try to be practical and logical. See every idea as enriching! Be hungry for ideas, welcome suggestions and evaluate later.

This is how it's done – For a lot of our lives we need routine, but it's a real killer when you are trying to be creative. We need to get into the habit of asking why things have always been done a certain way. For example, the QWERTY arrangement of keys on the keyboard was introduced to slow typists down when typewriters were new – they were going too fast and jamming the keys. Why do we still use that arrangement now? There's nothing to jam!

Don't be silly – This is probably what your parents have been telling you for the last ten years. Creativity needs a bit of silliness – we need to learn to play more.

I'm not creative – A survey was done to discover the difference between creative people and those who never came up with any new ideas. Was it because of social background, their education, their gender or age? The only difference found was that uncreative people labelled themselves with 'I'm not creative' – and so they weren't.

WHAT DOES THE BIBLE SAY ABOUT CREATIVITY?

Get a couple of members of your group to prepare and deliver a presentation on the wonders of the world around us. One tells what God made on each day of creation; the other comes up with some amazing facts that show the diversity and richness of the creation.

e.g. On the fifth day God created creatures that swim and birds that fly.

The blue whale is nearly 100ft long. Its tongue is ten foot thick. It has seven stomachs, arteries that you can swim through, a half-ton heart and eight tons of blood. Whales play for three times as long as they hunt for food.

Emphasise the richness and diversity of the world we live in, and the fact that God gave us this world to enjoy and develop. (Gen.1: 27-28) God gave us the ability to be creative too. Point out that the Bible, the story of God's dealings with people, starts in a garden (Eden) and ends with a city (The New Jerusalem in Revelation). God wants us to be creative, to develop what he's given us, to unlock the potential in creation.

DARTBOARD PROBLEM SOLVING

Use the list of twenty random words from the CDROM, and the Problem Solving page. Think of a problem facing your group: how to persuade the church to let them do a youth service, how to get their friends coming along. Write this at the centre of the Problem solving page. Get someone to throw a dart at the dartboard. The number they hit provides a word on your list. This is a trigger concept to help them approach the problem in a new way. Think about the word, explore its meaning and any associations. Try and make connections with the problem. Have a piece of paper with twenty circles on it. Try and fill each circle with an idea before you discard any.

Example: problem – fund-raising for an outing
            trigger concept – shoe.

What do shoes do? protect feet, keep them warm, look good, help you walk further, different shoes for different tasks, need cleaning, need replacing when worn out.

ideas: paid shoe-cleaning at church; helping people walk – deliver shopping, run errands; walk people's dogs; sponsored run/walk – I'm sure you can do better!

TALENT AUDIT

I'm sure you'll have done this before at some point but it bears repeating. Stick pieces of paper on everybody's backs. They should write their perceptions of each other's talents on the papers. Discuss in the group, add your own affirmations. What would they add to their own pieces of paper? It's very British to play down your gifts but it's very healthy to have a fair assessment of what you're good at and to enjoy it! Point out the range of gifts in the group.

THINGS THAT MAKE YOU GO 'WOW!'

We need to recover a sense of wonder, to pause to reflect on the diversity of the world, and the awesome creativity of God. Get group members to lie on their backs with their eyes closed. Encourage a hush, and then they should share things that make them go 'Wow!' e.g. taste of avocados, smell of earth after rain, winning a game of football, a bike ride, a good belly laugh.

Pray, thanking God for these things, for his creativity. Ask God to unlock creativity in each of your group, to enable them to glorify him.

Peace

When Jesus was born the angels sang that there would be peace on earth. The birth of Jesus gave people the opportunity to at last be fully at peace with God. We can know an amazing peace of mind through our relationship with him. But we are also called to be peacemakers, as Jesus made clear in his Sermon on the Mount, working to bring peace in situations of conflict. The meeting ready-to-use guide focuses more on the internal peace that knowing Jesus brings; the discussion starter focuses on the external peace that we need to work towards.

- 2003 saw the biggest demonstration in British history against war in Iraq. It's thought that around a million people turned up to march and make their views known. A BBC poll at the time showed that about 90 per cent of Britons were against the war and only 10 per cent supported the government view. When it came to a vote in the House of Commons, Labour won by a fair majority of 393 to 217 votes but suffered a big backbench rebellion with 139 MPs voting against the government in spite of a three-line whip. Many young people took part in anti-war protests, and these got a mixed reception. Some people were glad to see them politically engaged; others felt they were jumping on a bandwagon that they knew nothing about. See the note in the Stand Up introduction about Kierra Box and the Hands up for peace campaign.

Source: The Week, 22 February 2003

- There's a paradox in Jesus' teaching about peace. On the one hand he said in John 14:27 that he would leave his peace with the disciples when he returned to heaven. On the other he said, 'Do not suppose that I have come to bring peace to the earth. I did not come to bring peace, but a sword.' Jesus' whole ministry was in direct conflict with the powers of darkness; it's perhaps not surprising that when we see people coming into God's kingdom we'll experience some of that conflict. How would you explain this paradox to your group?

Some Bible passages:

Philippians 4:6,7 *In what ways does God's peace pass understanding?*

Matthew 5:9 *Have you ever brought peace to a troubled situation?*

Psalm 34:11-16 *'Seek peace and pursue it'; it doesn't sound like peace was ever meant to come easily. We need to be determined.*

Matthew 10:34-39 *Does this mean that some conflict is inevitable? Are there some situations where we should give up on trying to bring peace?*

Discussion starter Use the track *Peace on earth* from U2's album *All that you can't leave behind* (2000 Island). This album was created at a time when Bono was very involved in the Jubilee 2000 campaign and work with Amnesty International. The sleeve notes urge fans to join organisations working for justice such as Amnesty, Jubilee 2000, War Child and Greenpeace. As always the songs blend a passion for truth and justice with a gritty realism. The song *Peace on earth* was written in response to the Omagh bomb in August 1998 when Ireland suffered its greatest terrorist atrocity; 29 people and two unborn children were killed when a car bomb exploded in the town centre. The song lists some of the names of people killed by the bomb. Breda, who is mentioned, was a little girl, nearly two. Her mum, Tracey Devine had taken her into the town centre to buy her some shoes to wear to her uncle's wedding the following week, where she was to be a flower girl. Tracey suffered 65 per cent burns and was in a coma for six weeks. She was the last person to leave hospital after the bomb, and just made it home in time for Christmas that year.

Ask the group to list places in the world that need peace; you could write these up on a flip chart. Explain some of the background to the Omagh bomb and play the track to the group.

DISCUSS WITH THE GROUP:

● What emotions was Bono feeling when he wrote this song?

● Bono says that 'hope and history won't rhyme'; he perhaps feels that although God promised peace on earth when the angels came at Christmas, history shows that it won't happen. Do you agree with him?

55

Do you think we should work for peace in situations of conflict? Why? (see Mt. 5:9)

● What are some of the dangers of responding to violence like this with even more violence? Refer to the line 'and you become a monster so the monster will not break you.'

● Do you think this song shows a lack of faith in Jesus? Explain why.

● Can we pray for peace in situations like Northern Ireland? How might God act to bring peace?

After the discussion, you could play the track again and invite people to pray for the situations listed on the flipchart. You could give each person a coloured pen and as they pray, ask them to circle the name of the place with their pen, representing the way they are surrounding the situation with their prayers.

Source: The Guardian 23 December 1998

ON THE CDROM

● Peace sheet one – lateral thinking puzzles

● Peace sheet two – to help young people think about relationships with others.

GET READY

● Find a video of a conflict situation. It could be a film of a war/battle that is appropriate to the age of your group, or some suitable news footage on a loop. Alternatively find some newspaper or magazine articles about conflict and stick these around the room.

● Make one copy of Peace sheet one from the CDROM, and enough copies for everyone of Peace sheet two.

● You'll need magazines with lots of adverts of things that offer peace and relaxation such as holiday ads, aromatherapy oils, candles, chillout music, gardening, calm colours and so on, plus a large sheet of paper, glue and scissors for them to make a collage.

● Ask someone to practise reading John 14:23-27 so they can read it as if Jesus is speaking. This is a good way to involve older members of the group.

- You will also need a big bag of Skittles sweets, black pens or pencils, coloured pens, a CD player and some chillout music.

READY-TO-USE GUIDE

AIM: *To understand the nature of God's peace and how we can experience it*

GET YOUR BRAINS WORKING!

Lateral thinking puzzles need a style of problem-solving that involves looking at a given situation from unexpected angles, questioning the assumptions we are making about it.

Read out the puzzles from the sheet on the CDROM and see if anyone can work out the answers. Your group may know some other lateral thinking puzzles. Ask for their favourites.

THE WORLD'S PEACE

Introduce the subject. Give the group the magazines and ask them to make a collage or compile a list of ways in which the world offers peace. They could look out for holiday ads, aromatherapy oils, candles, chill-out music, gardening, calm colours. While they are doing this, put the conflict video on with the sound down or make sure the conflict pictures are visible.

Talk about the collages and how the world offers peace to people. Most of our associations are to do with escapism – getting away from stress and noise. Ask who noticed the video or pictures. The conflict was just as real, even though the sound was down, or they didn't notice the pictures and words. What kind of situations do they want peace in? Is it possible to find peace in the midst of conflict?

Paul talks in Philippians about the 'peace of God which passes understanding.' It's time to think laterally about peace, to think outside our normal assumptions and associations.

BIBLE STUDY

Ask someone to practice reading John 14:23-27 so they can read it as if Jesus is speaking. Ask the group to get comfortable and close their eyes; then set the scene. 'It's the Passover meal just before Jesus is crucified. The disciples are aware that something is going to happen, but haven't worked out exactly what. Jesus has washed their feet, taking the role of the servant. He has talked about the fact that one of them is going to betray him and Judas has left. He has told Peter that he will deny him, much to Peter's dismay. Now Jesus takes some time to pass on some really important words that he wants the disciples to remember. In the middle of it, he says the following:' Now get the person to read the passage.

The disciples were about to have their world turned upside down. But Jesus promises them peace in the midst of that. He wasn't talking about quietness or escaping what was about to happen. So what kind of peace was he talking about?

Pass round a bag of Skittles for people to help themselves. Explain that just as Skittles are multi-coloured (Taste the rainbow!), so the peace that Jesus is talking about is a rich, multi-faceted thing. The Hebrew word for peace is 'Shalom'. It means not just absence of conflict, but fulfilment and enjoyment – everything working as God intended, being right with God, other people and the creation. It is engaging with the world, not escaping from it. It is life in all its fullness, rather than life emptied of anything that we don't like.

Talk about these ideas. Ask the group how they would explain this concept of peace in a text message to a friend. See who can come up with the best text – this will show whether they have understood!

The disciples probably didn't experience much of this peace in the next few days after this meal. But it was certainly demonstrated at Pentecost, when the Spirit came.

BE FRUITY

Another way of explaining this peace is 'fruitfulness'. Give everyone a copy of Peace sheet two from the CDROM. Ask them to write their name on the figure in the centre and the names of four or five important people in their lives on the other figures – family, friends, enemies, they can choose. They also need a black pen or pencil each.

Now they should think about their relationship with each of those and imagine it is a plant! They should draw or write in between their name and each of the other names on their sheet, what type of plant the relationship represents. A good relationship could be a strong tree; a spiky relationship could be a cactus; a weak relationship could be a weed. It's probably most difficult for them to think about their relationship to the creation – do they have respect for what God has made? Are they making good use of the earth's resources? If they've never thought about it before they can just draw a little seed there – something that needs to grow!

The peace that Jesus gives is about being fruitful or flourishing in our relationships – enjoying other people, growing through our friendships, giving and receiving. We are called to be peacemakers – those who address conflict and try to put things right, not just smooth things over and escape from trouble. Receiving the peace that Jesus gives is about letting him into these relationships. Knowing that we are right with God and with others, and that we are loved, gives us a strong sense of well-being that will carry us through any conflict.

Think back to the situations that they wanted peace in. How will fruitful relationships help bring peace?

PRESS PAUSE

Peace can be found in the middle of noise. It is not necessarily about being quiet. But we do need to press pause at times in our busy lives, in order to receive what Jesus wants to give us. People will do this in different ways. Play some music and give people some space to pray about the relationships they have drawn on the sheet. Give them some coloured pens and ask them to draw their prayers – drawing the fruitfulness that they would like to see in these relationships by adding leaves, flowers, fruit, stronger stems etc, asking the Holy Spirit to transform them. End by praying for them all together and encourage them to go and do what they can to strengthen these relationships.

Expectations

Young people who heard a 'Come to Jesus and be happy' gospel won't have long to go before they realise that being a Christian is not like that. Having a right expectation of the Christian faith and of God is crucial so that disillusionment and anger don't set in. We also need to learn how to deal with other people's expectations of us – especially if we feel that they are holding us back. The ready-to-use guide attempts to do both – you can emphasise one over the other, according to the needs of your group. New Year is an obvious time to think about expectations – to look back over the last twelve months and forward to the next year, another good time is the start of a new school year.

● Talk with friends. What expectations did you have about what being a Christian would be like? Were those met? How do you cope with disillusionment and things going wrong? What expectations have others had of you in your life? How much influence have those had over you?

● Listen to *Driftwood* by Travis from the album *The Man Who*. Fran Healey wrote this song while he was washing up one evening. For some reason he was thinking about an episode of the American soap *Cheers* that he'd seen years and years earlier. One of the characters had commented that his boss was going to get rid of all the people in his office who were no good at their jobs, and he used the phrase 'clearing out all the driftwood'. The song is about someone who is thought to have wasted their life. Is there any sense of hope in the song? Jesus often spent time with people that society considered to be 'driftwood' – how has his example shaped your youth work?

Some Bible passages:

Psalm 27 *David is really confident of God's love and protection even in the midst of things going wrong. Is your experience of God the same?*

Luke 2:41-52 *Put yourself in Mary's shoes – what would you expect the Son of God to be like as a child? Is Jesus giving his relationship* *with God more priority than honouring his parents (Ex. 20:12)? How can you help young people to do both things, especially if there seems to be tension between the two?*

John 1:19-31 and Matthew 11:1-6 *You will look at John with the young people but his experience is worth thinking about in advance. What expectations do you think he had of Jesus as the Messiah? Why do you think he then questioned whether Jesus was the one? What do you think Jesus meant when he said, 'Blessed are those who don't fall away on account of me'?*

Discussion starter Show a clip from the film *Shrek* (cert PG). Shrek and Donkey are trying to rescue Princess Fiona from the tower where she is kept under guard by a fire-breathing dragon. The clip starts just after the dragon falls for Donkey and carries him off into the castle for some lurve. The clip ends when Shrek picks Princess Fiona up and throws her over his shoulder. Stop the tape after she says, 'This is not dignified. Put me down!'

Clip start time: 0:33:45
Clip end time: 0:41:45
Length of clip: eight minutes

● Fiona had a clear idea of who she thought would rescue her. What were her expectations of her 'knight in shining armour'? For those who know the film, what other expectations did she have in the film? Were these met?

● What expectations do other people have of you – in terms of how they think you should behave, or what job you might do in the future? Are these expectations helpful, or a hindrance?

● What expectations do you have of yourself?

● Is it good to have high expectations – to dream and imagine what life could be like, or is it better to aim low and then you're less likely to be disappointed?

ON THE CDROM

- Expectations sheet one – to help think about what expectations others have of us

- Expectations sheet two – Bible passages for your group to look at

GET READY

- Confound their expectations! Disturb the normal routine of your group session. If you normally have biscuits and coke, give them cake and coffee. If you are usually well dressed, come in your pyjamas and dressing gown. If every week you meet in a certain room, change the venue. How do they react? Do they like their expectations always to be met?

- Choose records for the Hit, Miss or Maybe session or ask some of your group to run that activity. Make 'thumbs up' signs or just ask them to give a signal with their hands.

- Make copies of Expectations sheet one from the CDROM, enough for one each; choose clothes to demonstrate how other people can have expectations of us.

- Make a copy of Expectations sheet two and cut into three.

- You need paper and envelopes, plus honey, breadsticks and lemon slices.

READY-TO-USE GUIDE

AIMS: *to consider what expectations others have of us and whether these are helpful or hinder us*

to make sure we have a right expectation of what life with Christ is like

HIT, MISS OR MAYBE?

Get some just-released singles and have a 'Hit, Miss or Maybe' session – you could draw 'thumbs up' signs on card which can also serve as 'thumbs down' for records they don't like. Play the single, discuss and vote. Try and choose groups that appeal to different people to get discussion going. What are their expectations for each single? How objective are they? Will loyalty stop them being honest? Alternatively, talk about football teams – who will win the premier league?

OTHER PEOPLE'S EXPECTATIONS

Give each of your group a copy of Expectations sheet one. Point out that different people in our lives will have different expectations of us. Illustrate by getting one of your group out the front and dressing them in different clothes. For example your parents may expect you to become a doctor (white coat, stethoscope, thermometer); your friends may expect you to support a particular team or do what they do (Chelsea football shirt and 18 video or cigarettes); you may feel God expects you to become a Christian worker (dog collar and vicar's robes). Get them to draw or write words around the first three figures to show what they feel each of those people expect of them.

Encourage them to spend longer thinking about what they expect from themselves, either short term over the next couple of years, or longer term when they become adults. What things will they have acquired? What activities do they think they will be doing? What people do they expect to have around them? What do they think they will be like when they reach the grand old age of 25?!

DISCUSSION

Discuss the sheets. Get them to share some of those expectations that they feel others put on them. Are they a help or a hindrance? Do they weigh them down or spur them on? How do the first three figures compare and contrast with each other? Which fits most closely with the expectations they have of themselves? What do the differences say about the relationships they have with those people and God?

Other people's expectations can either encourage us to do better, or actually hold us back. Remind them of the story of David and Goliath. When David offered to fight the giant, Saul made him try on his armour as Saul's expectation was that warriors wore armour. David found it much too big and it got in his way – so he went out as himself and you know the rest (1 Sam.17). You can use the dressed up group member as a further illustration. Get them to look at their figures – which of those expectations do they need to 'take off' because they are getting in the way? You obviously need to be sensitive where parental expectations are concerned – be prepared to talk to individuals from your group about this more later. Gently correct their wrong expectations of God and/or make a note to follow these up in later group sessions.

BIBLE STUDY

The focus of this Bible study is to look at their expectation of life with Christ.

Split the group into three and give each one of the following passages. Ask the group to read the passage and think about the following questions.

Matthew 11:1-6 John the Baptist

Matthew 19:16-22 The rich young ruler

Matthew 20:20-28 James and John

● What did this person expect from their relationship with Jesus?

● How do you think they felt after this encounter with Jesus?

● Would they give up on him because their expectations weren't met?

John the Baptist was disillusioned by what happened to him; his confidence that Jesus was the Messiah evaporated. (Contrast John 1:29-34 with the passage given.) The rich young ruler was expecting rules to obey, not costly lifestyle choices and James and John were expecting glory.

To avoid becoming disillusioned with the Christian life, we need to make sure we have the right expectations. What did Jesus tell his followers to expect? Ask one person to read John 10:7-10 and another to read John 16:33. The second passage is Jesus speaking to his disciples just before he leaves them – you may want to read a bit more to give the context.

Jesus seems to be contradicting himself – on the one hand he is promising life in its fullness and on the other he is promising trouble. What's going on? Introduce the idea of paradox – two seemingly contradictory statements that are both true at the same time. Jesus promises an abundant life, but not a pain-free one. Discuss how this is possible. Douglas Coupland wrote 'Adventure without risk is Disneyland' – what does that mean in relation to these words of Jesus?

Any achievement worth having takes effort and energy. God does give us the free gift of eternal life but wants us to work to bring in his kingdom

– not sit back and wait for it to happen. Use examples from your life – about the good things God has done for you, but also about times of struggle that have helped you learn, or brought you closer to God.

LOOKING AHEAD

Ask the group to think about the coming year or term. What are their expectations? Give them a piece of paper and an envelope each. Ask them to write down one thing in each of the following categories:

- One thing I know will happen

- One good thing I hope will happen

- One bad thing I think might happen

- One dream I have

- One thing I want in my relationship with God

They should seal the paper in the envelope and write their name and the date on the front. You could collect the envelopes in to look after or ask them to keep them safe at home. Set a date at the end of the term or halfway through the year, when you will suggest they re-open the envelopes and see if they were right.

PRAYER

Have honey, breadsticks and slices of lemon available. Honey symbolises the sweet things in life – fun, enjoyment, achievement, love – and lemon the bitter things – struggles, disappointment, hard work, pain. Both kinds of experiences are entwined in the abundant life Jesus brings and he is with us through it all. Encourage them to take some of each, if they can, to show they are willing to embrace what Jesus has to offer – but they also need to be honest. If they only want the good things they should just have some honey! As they eat they can pray about the things they have just written down.

Pray for them that they will have high expectations of life with Christ, and they will be able to overcome the difficulties ahead and enjoy life in all its fullness.

Read Ephesians 3:17b – 21 as a prayer over them.